W9-BNO-269

MEXICO

SCHAUMBURG TOWNSHIP DISTRICT LIBRARY
130 SOUTH ROSELLE ROAD
SCHAUMBURG, ILLINOIS 60193

EDWARD PARKER

Facts On File, Inc.

10/04
707
$30

TITLES IN THE COUNTRIES OF THE WORLD SERIES:
AUSTRALIA • BRAZIL • CHINA • EGYPT • FRANCE • GERMANY • ITALY JAPAN • KENYA • MEXICO • UNITED KINGDOM • UNITED STATES

Mexico

3 1257 01660 1162

Copyright © 2004 by Evans Brothers Limited

All rights reserved. No part of this book may be reproduced or utilized in any form or by any means, electronic or mechanical, including photocopying, recording, or by any information storage or retrieval systems, without permission in writing from the publisher. For information contact:

Facts On File, Inc.
132 West 31st Street
New York NY 10001

Library of Congress Cataloging-in-Publication Data

Parker, Edward, 1961–
  Mexico / Edward Parker.
    p. cm. — (Countries of the world)
  Includes index.
  ISBN 0-8160-5503-3 (hc)
    1. Mexico—Juvenile literature. I. Title. II. Countries of the world (Facts On File, Inc.)

F1208.5.P35 2004
972—dc22   2004047098

Facts On File books are available at special discounts when purchased in bulk quantities for businesses, associations, institutions, or sales promotions. Please call our Special Sales Department in New York at (212) 967-8800 or (800) 322-8755.

You can find Facts On File on the World Wide Web at http://www.factsonfile.com.

Printed in China by Imago

10 9 8 7 6 5 4 3 2 1

Endpapers (front): Cacti thrive on the edge of a lake in Baja California.
Title page: Children play in the sulfurous water at Hieve El Agua, Oaxaca state.
Imprint and Contents page: Desert landscapes of Baja California.
Endpapers (back): A view of Mexico City at night.

Editor: Katie Orchard
Designer: Jane Hawkins
Map artwork: Peter Bull
Charts and graphs: Encompass Graphics Ltd.
Photographs: all by Edward Parker
                      except front endpapers
                      (Corbis Digital Stock); 31
                      (Jon Spaull)

First published by Evans Brothers Limited,
2A Portman Mansions, Chiltern Street, London
W1U 6NR, United Kingdom.

This edition published under license from Evans Brothers Limited. All rights reserved.

CONTENTS

WITHDRAWN

The Mexican flag has three vertical bands of green, white and red. The green band represents hope; white stands for purity; and red represents the blood of national heroes. In the center is the Mexican coat of arms.

Mexico City is one of the largest cities in the world and a major commercial center.

Mexico is a very large country. It is the third largest in Latin America, after Brazil and Argentina, and it is the largest Spanish-speaking nation in the world. It covers an area of nearly 2 million km², which is approximately one quarter of the size of the United States. Mexico is the only country in the world that has frontiers with a superpower and with developing nations.

THE SHAPE OF MEXICO

Roughly triangular in shape, Mexico is widest in the north, where it shares a 2,400km border with the United States. Toward the south, it gradually narrows as far as the Isthmus of Tehuantepec, where it is only 215km wide. Below this point the country broadens out again at the Yucatán Peninsula and the Chiapas highlands, where it shares a 845km border with its southern neighbors, Belize and Guatemala.

1. MÉXICO
2. MORELOS
3. TLAXCALA
4. AGUASCALIENTES
5. QUERÉTARO
6. GUANAJUATO
7. PUEBLA
8. COLIMA
9. DISTRITO FEDERAL

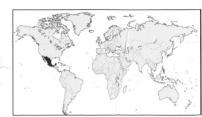

Mexico has a population of almost 100 million people. About 33 percent of the population are under the age of 15.

A DIVERSE COUNTRY

Mexico is a diverse country in terms of its landscapes and its people. Mexico's population is hugely varied. There are more than 50 distinct indigenous groups, and a rich mixture of people descended from both indigenous groups and the various waves of settlers that came to the country after the Spanish conquered it (see pages 22–23).

The economic fortunes of Mexico's people are equally varied. A small percentage of Mexicans live a life of luxury and privilege, while millions of poor people live in conditions that are shocking by any nation's standards. This striking rich-poor divide is surprising because Mexico is a highly industrialized nation that is rich in both natural and human resources. Mexico is one of the world's largest producers of oil and has huge reserves of industrial metals. The country also has a breathtaking landscape that attracts millions of tourists every year. However, Mexico also has a crippling foreign debt and many social problems, such as a high crime rate and lack of adequate healthcare. The country faces some serious environmental problems, too, with toxic air pollution in the capital, Mexico City, high rates of deforestation, expanding areas of desert and a lack of water in the north.

Mexicans are very proud of their country. Their ancient heritage stretches back more than 4,000 years and includes the great Aztec, Maya and Toltec cultures. The arrival of various groups of settlers has also left its mark on the country. Three hundred years as a Spanish colony have had a huge influence on Mexico, giving the country a strong Spanish culture that is still very noticeable today.

The Pyramid of Niches was built by the Totonac people between A.D. 600 and 700.

KEY DATA

Official Name:	The United States of Mexico
Area:	1,972,547km^2
Population:	98,881,000 (2000 census)
Main Cities:	Mexico City (capital), León, Guadalajara, Monterrey, Puebla
GDP Per Capita:	US$8,969*
Currency:	Mexican peso
Exchange Rate:	US$1 = 11 pesos £1 = 19 pesos

* Calculated on Purchasing Power Parity basis
Source: World Bank

Pico de Orizaba, Mexico's highest mountain, remains snow covered all year.

Mexico has a wide variety of different landscapes, including snow-capped volcanoes and mountains, tropical beaches, vast plateaux, peninsulas and huge deserts. Because it is such a vast country with a wide range of altitudes, Mexico's climate is also very varied, with cool plateaux, regions of high rainfall and high temperatures, and baking deserts.

COPPER CANYON

One of Mexico's most dramatic landmarks is a series of 20 canyons, carved out of the Western Sierra Madre by the Rio Urique. Together, these canyons cover an area four times larger than the Grand Canyon in the US state of Arizona. The deepest canyon, known as Urique, plunges down 1,879m, making it considerably deeper than the Grand Canyon. Barranca del Cobre, or Copper Canyon, is the most famous of the canyons because of the railway line that descends through it from Divisadero Barrancas in the mountains to the coastal city of Los Mochis.

A view of Copper Canyon from a train near Divisadero Barrancas.

LAND OF MOUNTAINS AND VOLCANOES

Mexico is a very mountainous country, with an average land height of 1,000m. Its two major landscape features are the Western Sierra Madre and Eastern Sierra Madre mountain ranges. Running roughly parallel to the coasts, they enclose the vast Mexican Plateau. These ranges rise to altitudes of 2,300m and form a major barrier between the central plateau and the coastal areas. In the Western Sierra Madre mountain range there are only two main transport routes from the Mexican Plateau across the mountains to the sea: the train line through Copper Canyon and the spectacular highway route from Durango to Mazatlán.

The Pacific states of Guerrero, Oaxaca and Chiapas are particularly mountainous and contain several other smaller mountain ranges. These include the Southern Sierra Madre, the Oaxaca Sierra Madre and the Soconusco mountains. Mexico is also a very volcanically active country. More than 200 seismic events, such as tremors, volcanic eruptions and earthquakes, are recorded in Mexico every year. At the southern edge of the Mexican Plateau is a rugged range of volcanic mountains known as the Transverse Volcanic mountain range, crossing the country roughly from east to west. It includes Mexico's most active volcano, Popocatépetl, and Mexico's newest volcano, Paricutín, which first appeared in 1943. Mexico's highest mountain, the snow-capped Pico de Orizaba, whose peak rises to 5,700m, is also found in the Transverse Volcanic mountain range. Much of Mexico's seismic activity occurs in this region. The most serious earthquake in recent years happened in Mexico City in 1986, killing more than 8,000 people.

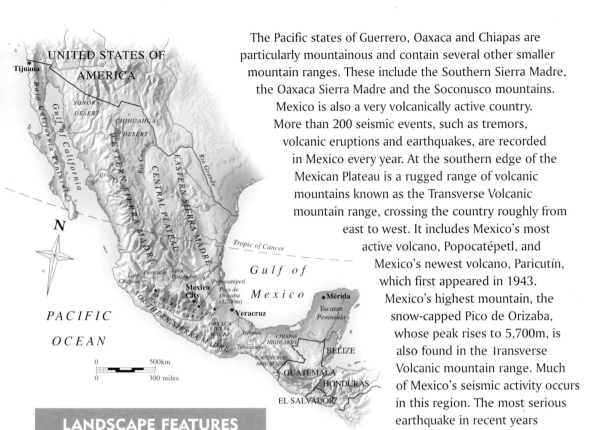

LANDSCAPE FEATURES

CASE STUDY
EL POPOCATÉPETL VOLCANO

Smoke rises from Popocatépetl during an eruption in 1997.

With its peak rising to 5,452m, Popocatépetl is Mexico's second-highest mountain. Its name in Nahuatl (the Aztec language) means "smoking mountain," in reference to the way it regularly puffs out sulfurous clouds of steam and smoke. Generally, its volcanic activity is gentle. However, occasionally Popocatépetl has spectacular eruptions that threaten the human populations living on its lower slopes. There have been 14 major eruptions since the time of the Spanish *conquistadores*, 500 years ago. In March 2003 a medium-sized eruption blasted ash more than 8km into the air, and molten lava ran down the volcano's steep slopes, forcing more than 25,000 people to be evacuated from the area.

Popocatépetl is only 72km southeast of Mexico City and 43km west of the city of Puebla. If a major eruption occurs, more than 30 million people will be under threat. The government's National Disaster Prevention Center constantly monitors the seismic activity and the composition of gases escaping from the volcano, in order to give advance warnings of possible eruptions.

ABOVE: A view of part of the vast tableland of the Mexican Plateau.
RIGHT: Horses drink at the shores of Lake Patzcuáro, one of Mexico's largest lakes.

EVOLVING LANDSCAPE

The current shape of Mexico and its landscape are the result of millions of years of geological activity. Mexico is volcanically active because it lies at the junction of two of the Earth's major continental plates. These plates form a jigsaw of landmasses that make up the Earth's crust, which floats on top of a layer of molten, moving rock called magma. These vast plates are always moving. Mexico's mountain ranges have been formed over millions of years by the slow collision of two plates called the North American Plate and the Cocos Plate. As these plates have pushed together, the landmasses have crumpled up, forming a series of mountain ranges. At the same time faults, or cracks, at the edges of these vast plates have allowed magma to rise to the Earth's surface, forming volcanoes.

THE MEXICAN PLATEAU

The Mexican Plateau is a vast high plateau, or tableland, situated between the Sierra Madre mountain ranges and the Transverse Volcanic Mountain Range. It runs northward from just south of Mexico City to beyond the US frontier. It covers approximately 1 million km^2 and comprises a mosaic of landscapes of vast, flat expanses, river valleys and low, rolling hills.

This central plateau can be divided into two distinct areas. The northern half of the Mexican Plateau is characterized by a gently sloping tableland with an average altitude of 1,000m. This extends north, crossing the US border into the states of Texas and New Mexico. This area includes North America's largest desert — the Chihuahua Desert. The southern half of the Mexican Plateau, where most Mexicans live, has an average altitude of over 2,000m. This area of high plateau is made up of low hills and broad valleys. Much of the most productive farmland in Mexico is found in this area.

A feature of the great Mexican Plateau are the bolsons (valleys that have no exit for water) and large lakes caused by the surrounding mountain ranges preventing rivers flowing to the sea. Lake Chapala in Jalisco state is Mexico's largest lake.

CASE STUDY
CHIHUAHUA DESERT

Sand ripples across the sand dunes of the Chihuahua Desert, near the US border.

The Chihuahua Desert covers an area of around 500,000km². Millions of years ago the whole area was on the seabed, but today it is raised up with an average altitude of over 1,000m. It comprises a vast plateau bordered by the Sierra Madre mountain ranges on either side. The plateau itself tilts toward the north-west with altitudes averaging 2,000m in the south and just 500m in Texas to the north. It is a desert of surprising landscape diversity with low hills, river valleys and even wetland areas. The average temperatures become increasingly colder toward the north. Regions on either side of the US border experience sharp frosts at night during the winter, and snowfalls are not uncommon. In the south, near cities such as San Luis Potosí, the desert experiences high temperatures (between 30–40°C in the summer) and receives only around 250mm of rain each year.

Tourists visit the sacred *cenote* at the ancient Maya city of Chichén Itzá.

COASTAL PLAINS AND PENINSULAS

Mexico's eastern coastline stretches for 2,780km along the Gulf of Mexico and the Caribbean Sea, from the US border to tropical Belize. The western coast is considerably longer, running for 7,360km along the Pacific Ocean from the US border to Guatemala. This is due to the indented coastline of the long, thin peninsula of Baja California. Inland from the coasts is a series of coastal plains of varying widths. The plains are at their widest in the northwest, in the states of Sonora and Sinaloa, where the landscape is typically desert or semi-desert. The coasts along the Gulf of Mexico are characterized by wide beaches, sandbars and swamps.

Mexico has two large peninsulas, Baja California and the Yucatán. Baja California juts out into the Pacific Ocean, extending south for about 1,200km from the border of the United States. This is a narrow strip of land with a series of small mountain ranges that run down its spine. The desert and semi-desert coastlines of Baja California are broken only by occasional oases.

The Yucatán Peninsula is a relatively flat area of land that juts out into the Gulf of Mexico. It has few visible rivers or lakes because the limestone bedrock is porous, allowing water to seep into it. However, huge rivers flow underground and the area is marked by *cenotes*, or sinkholes, formed when the roofs of underground river caverns collapse.

CLIMATE

Mexico is divided almost exactly in half by the tropic of Cancer. The land to the north is generally temperate and is affected by polar winds. In the south, the climate falls into the broad category of subtropical. Here, the prevailing winds are generally moist and warm and head up from the tropical south.

Mexico has a remarkable range of climatic conditions. The different climatic zones are defined according to altitude: *tierra caliente* or tropical (below 650m); *tierra templada* or temperate (650–2,000m); and *tierra fria* or cold (above 2,000m). There is an extensive area of *tierra caliente* bordering the Caribbean coast, including the whole of the Yucatán Peninsula, while only a thin strip of the Pacific coastline of Mexico falls into this category. As more than two-thirds of Mexico are dominated by mountains and high plateaux, most of the country falls into the categories of *tierra templada* and *tierra fria*. Most areas of *tierra fria* experience night frosts in the winter, although snowfall only settles above 3,000m.

HURRICANE PAULINA

The west and east coasts of Mexico are occasionally affected by tropical storms, which develop in the Pacific or Caribbean and bring two or three days of heavy rain. These occur mainly during August, September and October. A few storms develop into hurricanes. One of the most severe in recent decades was Hurricane Paulina, which ravaged the southwest coast of Mexico in October 1997. The torrential rains caused major landslides and extensive flooding, killing more than 2,500 people.

Mexico experiences distinct wet and dry seasons. The rainy season over the whole country coincides with the highest temperatures, between May and October. The wettest part of the country is the lowland of the Caribbean coast. Some areas have an annual rainfall of more than 5m. However, the average annual rainfall for these lowlands is 1,000–1,500mm, with the exception of a small area of northern Yucatán that is very arid, receiving less than 500mm each year. The northern coastal plains of the Pacific and Gulf of California are very dry, receiving less than 250mm of rainfall each year. Farther south along the Pacific coast the rainfall is higher, with 1,000–1,500mm each year in the states of Oaxaca and Chiapas. Generally, Mexico can be divided into the arid north and moist south.

This is one of a number of arid islands in the Gulf of California.

TEMPERATURE AND RAINFALL

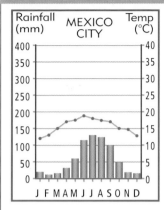

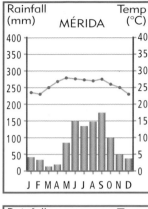

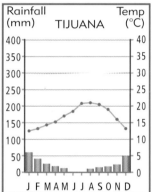

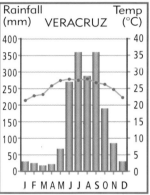

KEY:

Temp (°C)   Rainfall (mm)

15

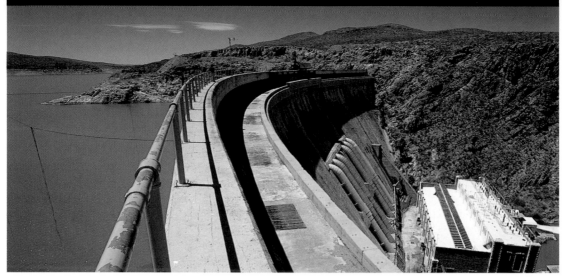

ABOVE: This HEP dam is on the Rio Conchos, near the city of Chihuahua.
RIGHT: This oil refinery in the state of Tabasco processes oil from the Gulf of Mexico.

The Spanish *conquistadores* (see pages 22–23) were first attracted to Mexico by rumors of spectacular wealth, and they were not disappointed. Mexico has an abundance of natural resources, including precious metals such as gold and silver and huge deposits of valuable minerals and oil. It has spectacular natural wealth, including the rich fisheries off its Pacific and Atlantic coasts and vast areas of native pine forests. Mexico also has a remarkable diversity of wildlife.

ENERGY

In 2001, Mexico was the world's sixth-largest oil producer, averaging 3.11 million barrels a day. Oil has been Mexico's single most important export for more than 50 years and the country looks set to be a major producer beyond 2020. The main reserves are located offshore in the Gulf of Mexico, accounting for about 56 percent of the country's oil. Mexico's other main reserves are near Chicontepec (24 percent) and in the states

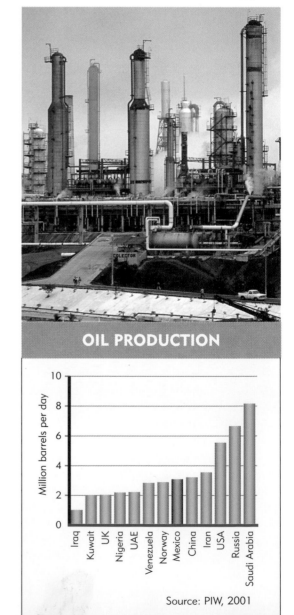

OIL PRODUCTION

Million barrels per day

Country	Production
Iraq	1
Kuwait	2
UK	2
Nigeria	2.2
UAE	2.2
Venezuela	2.8
Norway	2.9
Mexico	3.1
China	3.2
Iran	3.5
USA	5.5
Russia	6.6
Saudi Arabia	8.2

Source: PIW, 2001

of Chiapas and Tabasco (15 percent). Mexico also has large deposits of coal and gas.

In addition to fossil fuels, the country has a wide range of alternative energy sources. Around half of Mexico's power stations use oil to produce electricity, while a further third use hydroelectric power (HEP). Mexico also has geothermal, natural gas and nuclear power stations. Mexico's energy resources are so abundant that the country is able to export electricity and gas to the United States.

PRECIOUS METALS

The spectacular wealth of Mexico first reported to King Carlos I of Spain by the *conquistador* Hernan Cortéz was no exaggeration. Gold and silver from Aztec and other civilizations of Mexico made the Spanish king fabulously rich.

Today Mexico is the world's largest producer of silver, which is mined mainly in the states of Zacatecas and Chihuahua. Mexico boasts the world's largest silver mine at Minera Real de Angeles and accounts for around 20 percent of total world production. In 2000 Mexico produced 2,572,000kg of silver. Mexico's gold production is more modest, but the country still processed 24,535kg of gold in 2000.

INDUSTRIAL METALS

Mexico has abundant resources of industrial metals, which are exploited for use in many industrial processes. Iron, copper, zinc and lead are all mined in Mexico. The main areas of iron mining are in the states of Durango, Nuevo León and Coahuila, all in the north of the country. Mexico is also one of the world's largest producers of lead. Zinc is often found in association with lead, and most of it is exported to other countries. Copper, mined since pre-Hispanic times, is another metal essential to many of Mexico's industries. The main areas of copper production today include the states of Sonora, Chihuahua, Zacatecas and Michoacán. There are also deposits of rarer metals such as antimony, arsenic, bismuth and mercury, which are used in alloys and industrial processes.

MINING AREAS

Tijuana

UNITED STATES OF AMERICA

Gulf of California

Ciudad Juárez

Chihuahua

Los Mochis

Durango

Monterrey

Mazatlán

N

Guadalajara
León

San Luis Potosí

Mexico City

Puebla Veracruz

Acapulco

Oaxaca

PACIFIC OCEAN

Gulf of Mexico

Cancún
Mérida

Caribbean Sea

BELIZE

GUATEMALA

HONDURAS

EL SALVADOR

0   500km
0   300 miles

Precious and industrial metals
(gold, silver, lead, zinc, manganese, mercury)

Metals/minerals for iron and steel industries
(iron, titanium, tin)

Industrial minerals
(lead, zinc, mercury, antimony, tungsten, tin)

Copper

Salt is collected from a lagoon on the Yucatán Peninsula.

MINERALS

Mexico has many nonmetallic minerals, with large deposits of sulfur in Veracruz, Chiapas, Michoacán and Tamaulipas. Sulfur is used to make sulfuric acid, which is essential for industrial processes such as paper-making and in the refining of petroleum. Mexico is also the world's main producer of fluorite, celestite and sodium sulfate, much of which is exported around the world. The largest reserves of these minerals are located in San Luis Potosí, Coahuila, Chiapas, Guanajuato and Durango.

In addition to these minerals, Mexico is a major producer of graphite and barite. Salt is also found in large quantities, extracted from the sea along the coastlines or from the closed basins in the center of the country. Despite Mexico's wealth of mineral resources, they accounted for only 0.3 percent of the country's exports in 2000.

FOREST PRODUCTS

Vast pine and oak forests are found in northern and central Mexico. Trees in these areas are cut down and used primarily in the construction, paper and packaging industries.

This rain forest timber has been harvested outside the town of Chetumal.

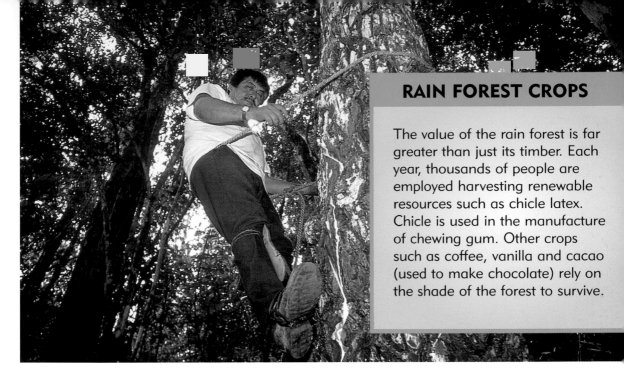

RAIN FOREST CROPS

The value of the rain forest is far greater than just its timber. Each year, thousands of people are employed harvesting renewable resources such as chicle latex. Chicle is used in the manufacture of chewing gum. Other crops such as coffee, vanilla and cacao (used to make chocolate) rely on the shade of the forest to survive.

The sticky sap from the chicle tree is harvested by hand and used as one of the ingredients in chewing gum.

However, the native forests of Mexico have been overharvested and there is concern about the long-term future of this resource. Poor planning and insufficient replanting programs mean that timber production is unsustainable. Trees take many years to mature and cannot be replaced quickly enough. Mexico also has significant areas of rain forest in the south, especially in the state of Chiapas. These, too, have been overharvested. Mexico may soon have to import timber and other forest products.

WATER

One resource that is vital to the people and economy of Mexico is water. However, the country's water resources are very unevenly distributed. The north has very little rainfall. For decades, water has been extracted from large underground reservoirs called aquifers. This underground water is being overexploited and lack of water is set to be a major problem in the future (see case study on page 50). In contrast, the south has abundant water resources, and the states of Chiapas, Tabasco and Veracruz can receive as much as 5.5m of rain each year. It is here that the abundant, swift-flowing rivers are exploited to produce HEP.

CASE STUDY
A DELICATE BALANCE

In the village of Ixtapeje, in Oaxaca state, a community of Zapotec Indians is reaping the benefit of not cutting down the forest.

In the past, many of the forest areas around the city of Oaxaca were cut down by local people, who sold the timber to supplement their incomes. However, cutting down too many trees can upset the delicate balance of nature. In areas of dense forest cover, rain is absorbed by the tree roots, other plants, and the soil, and then gradually released throughout the year. But in areas of deforestation the rainwater runs away more quickly, causing erosion and devastating flash floods.

By protecting the native pine and oak forest on their land, the villagers of Ixtapeje have ensured that there is water flowing in the small local streams all year round, in contrast to other nearby villages. The villagers supplement their incomes by bottling and selling their fresh water.

A group of fishermen in the Yucatán inspect the day's catch.

FISHERIES

Mexico has more than 10,000km of coastline and access to some of the most productive inland fisheries in the world. However, Mexico is not a major fishing nation, and therefore its fish stocks are likely to have a better future than those of European countries, which are quickly overexploiting their own stocks. Among the main types of fish caught are tuna, shrimp, sardine and squid. The most valuable of these in terms of export is shrimp.

GENETIC RESOURCES

Mexico also has many important genetic resources that may prove valuable to world agriculture in the future. It is the center of genetic diversity for many of the world's most important crops. By far the most important in terms of feeding the world is Mexico's diversity of maize, or corn, varieties. The country has hundreds of types of maize, developed over thousands of years to cope with local conditions such as drought or insect pests. Genetic material from the wild

relatives of major crops have been used all around the world to improve yields in crops such as maize. Other important crops that originated in Mexico include vanilla, cacao, chilies, jojoba and oregano. Mexico also has many native plants that have major potential as future food crops or medicines, such as palm fruits and a variety of edible and medicinal cacti.

NATURAL WEALTH

Mexico has a number of natural resources on which no economic value can be placed and others whose value is difficult to calculate. For example, the stunning landscapes of rugged mountains, deserts, tropical rain forests and golden beaches attract millions of tourists every year, earning hundreds of millions of dollars. Mexico also has more than 10 percent of all the world's species of birds, mammals and reptiles. Because of its rich biodiversity, Mexico is one of the most important countries in the world in terms of wildlife conservation. Its rich coastal waters provide feeding and breeding grounds for some of the world's rarest sea mammals.

CASE STUDY
WHALE WATCHING

The coastal waters of Mexico and especially the Gulf of California are the richest in the world in terms of whale and porpoise diversity. Whales such as the blue whale are often seen in the Pacific waters close to Mexico, and the gray whale breeds in the sheltered lagoons along the coastline of Baja California. Originally, whales were a natural resource hunted by whaling communities for products such as baleen (now replaced by plastics) and blubber. Today, these magnificent creatures are much more valuable as tourist attractions. Thousands of people visit Baja California for the opportunity to see the gentle giants at close quarters, providing a valuable income for local communities.

CANDELILLA

Candelilla is a small shrub that grows wild in the Chihuahua Desert. The plant is full of wax, which prevents water loss in the desert heat. When lit, the wax burns just like a candle, hence the name, which means "little candle" in Spanish. Local people pick the plant and collect the wax. It is then processed and sold internationally as an ingredient of many of the most popular shoe polishes and car waxes. The wax is also used to coat lemons, giving them a healthy-looking shine and a longer shelf life.

Candelilla harvesting provides an income for thousands of people who live in the Chihuahua Desert.

Mexico's rain forests have provided some of the world's most important crops.

MEXICO'S WILD SIDE

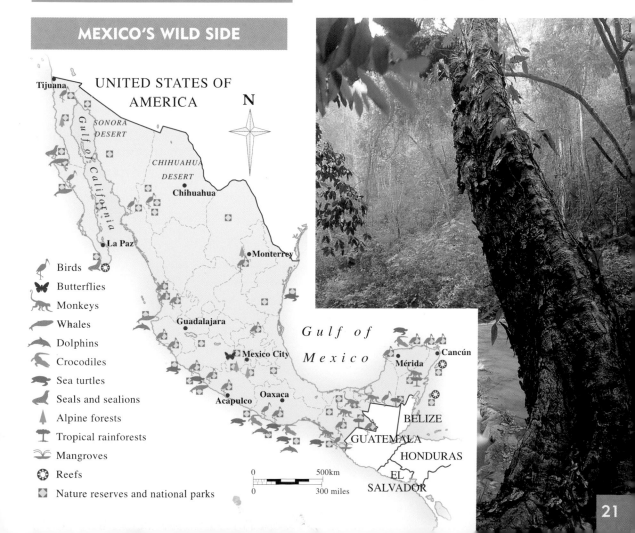

UNITED STATES OF AMERICA

N

Tijuana

Gulf of California

SONORA DESERT

CHIHUAHUA DESERT

Chihuahua

La Paz

Monterrey

Birds
Butterflies
Monkeys
Whales
Dolphins
Crocodiles
Sea turtles
Seals and sealions
Alpine forests
Tropical rainforests
Mangroves
Reefs
Nature reserves and national parks

Guadalajara

Mexico City

Gulf of Mexico

Cancún
Mérida

Acapulco

Oaxaca

BELIZE

GUATEMALA

HONDURAS

EL SALVADOR

0   500km
0   300 miles

Mexicans take in the view of Mexico City from Chapultepec Park.

Mexico's population has grown rapidly over the last 50 years, rising from 25.8 million in 1950 to 98.9 million by 2000. As a result, the country now has a young population with more than one third of people under the age of 15. The population is not equally spread throughout the country but varies greatly from region to region. Migration from the countryside to the cities now means that around a quarter of all Mexicans live in the capital, Mexico City.

FIRST PEOPLES AND THE *CONQUISTADORES*

Mexico is sometimes called "the country of 10,000 ruined cities." It was once home to some of the world's greatest civilizations. A succession of these flourished in Mexico between 1200 B.C. and A.D. 1519. The Olmecs, Maya, Zapotecs and Aztecs built great pyramids and cities, many of which are still visible today. Their societies were well organized and, in many ways, more advanced than other civilizations living in Europe at the same time. These cultures reached high levels of artistic and scientific achievement that influenced not only the cultures of Central America but also the development of human knowledge throughout the world. For example, by the time of Christ, the Maya had already developed highly accurate ways of measuring time. They had calculated that each year comprised 365.2422 days and that the Moon's orbit took 29.5209 days. It was not until the twentieth century that Western mathematicians could calculate more accurate figures.

The last great indigenous civilization to dominate Mexico was that of the Aztecs, which appeared in the early fourteenth century.

ABOVE: Teotihuacán was Mexico's largest ancient city. It also holds the world's third-largest pyramid.
RIGHT: A young man stands proudly in front of a monument to the Maya people, in Mérida.

At their peak, the Aztecs controlled most of central Mexico, an area approximately the size of Italy. However, this highly sophisticated civilization came to an abrupt end soon after the arrival of the Spanish *conquistador* Hernan Cortéz and his small army in 1519. Cortéz cleverly persuaded other Mexican Indian groups, who were attempting to resist the spread of the Aztec Empire, to join forces and overthrow them. They managed to do this, only to fall under the control of the Spanish.

POPULATION CRASHES

Cortéz's triumph marked the beginning of the colonial era. Spain controlled Mexico for the next 300 years. The initial period of colonization was devastating for the indigenous people of Mexico, bringing with it slavery, war and new diseases from Europe that wiped out huge numbers of people. It is estimated that at the start of the sixteenth century there were about 25 million indigenous people living in the regions known today as Mexico and Central America. Less than 100 years later this number had been reduced by 90 percent.

Mexico gained independence from Spain in 1821. But the country's troubles were not over, and Mexico soon found itself at war with the United States (1846–48). Thousands of soldiers were killed and more than half of Mexico's territory was lost. By 1910 the population of Mexico stood at 15 million people. The following year the Mexican Revolution started. This was a bloody conflict between the armies of a variety of leaders who wanted to govern Mexico. Within seven years, more than 1 million Mexicans had lost their lives.

REDRAWING THE MEXICAN MAP

Mexico was once a vast country that included a large part of what are now Central America and the United States. In the early nineteenth century North American settlers moved into the Mexican state of Texas. By 1836 they had declared Texas an independent republic and withstood the Mexican Army's efforts to reassert authority. By 1845 the US Congress had voted to annex Texas. This led to the Mexican-American War. Mexico was defeated and forced to sign the Treaty of Guadalupe Hidalgo in 1848, handing over the states of Texas, California, Nevada, Utah, Colorado and almost all of New Mexico and Arizona. By 1853 Mexico had lost almost half its territory when the remaining parts of the states of New Mexico and Arizona not already controlled by the United States were sold to that country for US$10 million.

MEXICANS TODAY

Today, the majority of Mexico's population is made up of people of native Mexican Indian and European descent, or *mestizos*. The main division in Mexican society is between indigenous people and *mestizos*. The indigenous people are the direct descendants of the original inhabitants of Mexico, who have retained a distinct sense of their cultural identity. *Mestizos* typically have both Mexican Indian and European heritage, but in areas such as the state of Veracruz the local population is also partly descended from Africans brought to Mexico as slaves during the eighteenth century. Over the last 200 years people from all over the world have migrated and settled in Mexico, including many Chinese people and people from Arab countries such as Lebanon. This great mixture of indigenous, European and other cultures has enabled Mexico to develop its own unique character.

MEXICO'S INDIGENOUS POPULATION

In modern Mexico the native Mexican Indian population has grown to almost 10 million. The largest indigenous group in Mexico includes the descendants of the Aztecs, called the Nahua. They have a population of over 1.7 million. The Nahua live in the central states of the country and most continue to use their traditional language, *Nahuatl*. In the south there are 800,000 Mayan speakers, descended from the great Maya civilization that once occupied much of south Mexico and Central America. The Zapotecs and Mixtecs each have populations of over 500,000. However, the populations of many other indigenous groups have become seriously reduced. Peoples such as the Seri people of the Sonoran Desert now number only a few hundred.

The Tarahumara people of northern Mexico are traditionally nomadic herders and hunters.

A group of Mayan women enjoy a visit to the amusement park in Mérida.

In total there are 56 distinct recognized indigenous groups in Mexico and as many as 139 indigenous languages have been recorded. However, over the last decade, the number of people over five years old who speak an indigenous language instead of Spanish has fallen from 7.5 percent to 7.1 percent of the population. The number of people who speak indigenous languages differs from state to state. For example, more than a third of the population of the states of the Yucatán and Oaxaca are native-language speakers; by contrast, states such as Zacatecas have virtually no native language speakers at all.

Many of the indigenous peoples of Mexico observe ancient religions and follow traditional agricultural lifestyles, such as growing maize and respecting the natural world around them.

More than a million Zapotec Indians live in the mountainous region of northern Oaxaca.

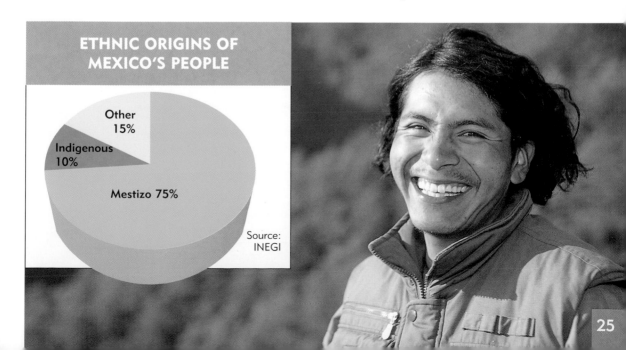

ETHNIC ORIGINS OF MEXICO'S PEOPLE

Other 15%

Indigenous 10%

Mestizo 75%

Source: INEGI

POPULATION GROWTH

Mexico's population has grown from just 13.5 million in 1900 to 99 million in 2000. Over the last hundred years there have been a number of distinct phases in Mexico's population growth. In 1900 the population was increasing at around 1 percent a year but by 1917 more than a million Mexicans had died in the Mexican Revolution. Soon after the end of the Revolution the population began to grow rapidly once more, and in 1965 Mexico had the fastest-growing population of any country in the world, at 3.4 percent annually.

During the last 30 years the growth rate of the Mexican population has been slowing down. By 2000 the annual growth rate had fallen to 1.85 percent. Although this is a significant reduction in the growth of the population it still means that a large number of babies are born every year in Mexico.

The population growth across the country varies greatly. While the average population growth for the country is about 2 percent, the populations of states such as Quintana Roo and Baja California have grown by about 6 percent and 4 percent respectively. These figures are partly the result of migrants moving into these states in search of better employment.

DISTRIBUTION

Mexico is a densely populated country, with 46 people per hectare compared with 28 people per hectare in the United States. However, Mexico's people are very unevenly distributed. For example, a quarter of all Mexicans live in Mexico City and half live in the fertile states within 200km of the capital.

There is also a marked contrast in the percentage of the population that lives in urban areas compared with rural areas. The 2000 census showed that only 25 percent of the population lived in settlements with fewer than 2,500 people. In contrast, nearly half of the population lived in urban areas with a population of 100,000 or more. Since 1950 the percentage of Mexican people living in urban areas has grown from just 43 percent to 74 percent.

POPULATION STRUCTURE

The massive population growth in recent years has led to a situation where around one third of Mexico's population is aged 15 or less. This "bottom-heavy" population structure puts enormous pressure on the country to provide new schools and social services and to create millions of new jobs in the next decade.

Nearly 1.8 million new babies are born in Mexico each year.

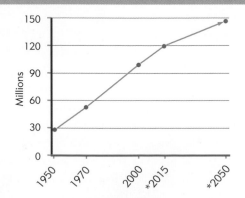

POPULATION GROWTH

Sources: UN Population Division, *Geographical Digest* and UNDP (* These figures are estimates)

However, the structure of the Mexican population is already beginning to change. The birth rate has fallen and life expectancy has been increasing over the last decade. If this trend continues, the population structure should become closer to that found in the United States or the United Kingdom.

POPULATION DENSITY

Cities with highest population densities

Population density
(number of people per km²)

- Over 500
- 100 to 499
- 50 to 99
- 10 to 49
- under 10

POPULATION STRUCTURE

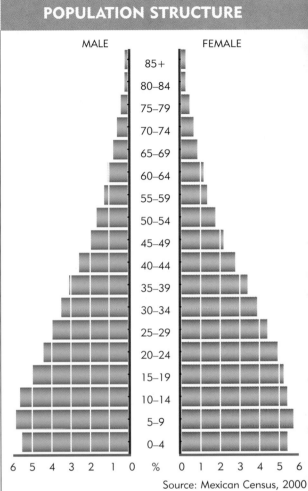

Source: Mexican Census, 2000

CASE STUDY
MEXICO CITY

Dramatic high-rise buildings tower over the commercial center of Mexico City.

With an official population of 18.7 million and covering nearly 2,000km², Mexico City is a megacity – one of the three largest in the world. More than half of all internal migrants head for Mexico City, and now nearly a quarter of all Mexicans live in this vast, sprawling city. Many arrive with little or no money and often end up living in the slum settlements that surround the capital. Many experts believe that the real population of Mexico City, including all the unofficial settlements around the city could exceed 24 million. At the heart of the city is the *Distrito Federal* (DF), which accounts for around half of the population. The remainder of the city spills out into México state, which surrounds the DF on three sides, and Morelos state.

INTERNAL MIGRATION

Mexicans often migrate within the country in search of a better standard of living. Over the last 50 years, huge waves of migrants have left the countryside and headed for the large cities to look for work or because they have been forced off their land. This migration from rural to urban areas is typical of most developing nations. Today there are a number of states in Mexico where the population is falling as people move away from rural areas. The main destinations have traditionally been Mexico City, Guadalajara and Monterrey. More recently, however, the northern cities of Ciudad Juárez, Chihuahua and Tijuana have attracted migrants because of opportunities in the new maquiladora industries (see pages 40–41). These industries are the fastest-growing part of the Mexican economy, providing thousands of new jobs every year.

MAIN PICTURE: In many rural areas of Oaxaca there are no roads. The main form of transporting goods is by horse or donkey. INSET: This suburb of Oaxaca City has grown up rapidly over the last 15 years.

The states gaining the most migrants are Quintana Roo (53.4 percent) and Baja California (49.5 percent). The state of Quintana Roo includes the rapidly growing tourist destination of Cancún, which has generated thousands of new jobs in the state over the last 20 years. Baja California is home to major tourist resorts and maquiladora industries. Baja California also includes the city of Tijuana, which is a major entry point for Mexicans as they head for the United States, either legally or illegally.

GROWTH OF URBAN POPULATION

y-axis: % of total (40, 45, 50, 55, 60, 65, 70, 75, 80)
*x-axis: 1950, 1970, 2000, *2015*

Sources: *Geographical Digest* and UNDP
*estimated figures

The slums of Tijuana extend right up to the metal fence that marks the border between Mexico and the United States.

Many of the poorest states have declining populations. Some states are losing huge numbers of young people as they leave the home areas in search of a better quality of life for themselves and their families. States such as Zacatecas and Durango have low population increases of just 0.59 percent and 0.72 percent respectively. People are moving away from these states in search of work because the main industries of mining and agriculture (which is suffering from desertification) are in decline.

INTERNATIONAL MIGRATION

Over the past 50 years, millions of Mexicans have migrated to the United States. In 2000 the number of US residents of Mexican origin was estimated to be around 7 million. Each year, thousands of Mexicans enter the United States, desperate to escape poverty. In 2000 nearly 174,000 Mexicans migrated legally to the United States. However, two to three times as many Mexicans enter the United States illegally each year, too.

POLICING THE US BORDER

Between October 1999 and September 2000, 1.6 million people were arrested while illegally trying to cross the border from Mexico into the United States. This figure is actually much higher than the real number of people trying to gain entry because many people made several attempts to enter the United States. Between October 2000 and September 2001 the number of Mexicans arrested trying to cross the border illegally had fallen to 330,325. Around 200,000 Mexicans migrate legally to the United States every year, although the estimated number of illegal immigrants living there in 2000 was 4.8 million.

Many people from other Central American countries migrate into Mexico in order to escape war, poverty and human rights abuses. Estimates suggest that there are about 45,000 Guatemalan refugees in southern Mexico. It is also estimated that a further 40,000–60,000 people from Guatemala cross the border each autumn to work on Mexico's coffee harvest. At the end of the season most of these people return to Guatemala.

Millions of Mexicans live in poverty conditions, like this family in Baja.

SOCIAL INDICATORS

UNDER-FIVE MORTALITY RATE

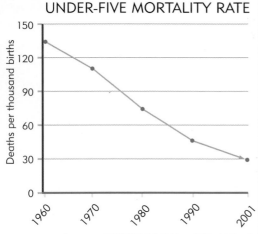

Sources: UNICEF, UNDP and World Bank

LIFE EXPECTANCY (YEARS)

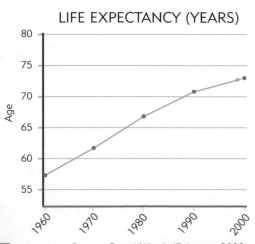

Source: Social Watch (February 2003)

In the last 50 years Mexico has changed from being a largely agricultural society to a country where the majority of the population now lives in urban areas. This has had a profound effect on the daily life of modern Mexicans. Over the same period of time the life expectancy has risen sharply, resulting from improved diets and better healthcare. However, despite these improvements millions of Mexicans still live in poverty.

AN UNEQUAL SOCIETY

Although Mexico is one of the world's 20 richest countries, its wealth is very unevenly distributed and there are vast differences between rich and poor lifestyles. For example, some residential areas in Mexico have homes similar to those of the wealthiest families in the United States and Europe. At the same time, millions of people do not have permanent homes and their lives resemble those of people in the poorest developing countries. All the major cities of Mexico have *pueblos jovenes* (urban slums). By far the largest number of slum settlements are in Mexico City, where it is estimated that around 30 percent of its inhabitants live in *pueblos jovenes*. Large differences in Mexican people's

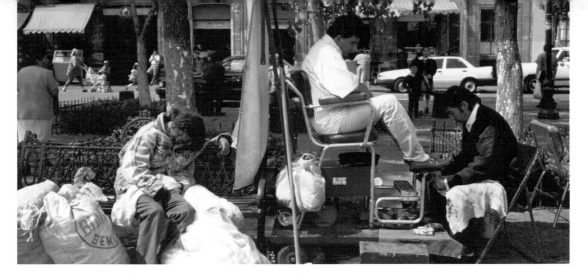

The rich-poor divide: A wealthy Mexican has his shoes shined only feet away from a homeless person living below the poverty line.

lifestyles exist not just between the rich and poor, but also between people living in urban and rural areas.

HEALTH

Today the proportion of people in Mexico that are 14 years old or under is still around one third of the population, but this is gradually getting smaller as Mexican families have fewer children and live longer. Between 1970 and 2000 the life expectancy rose from 61 to 73 years. This increase was largely due to improved diets and better healthcare. Since 1970 the infant mortality rate (the number of children who die in the first year of life) has also fallen, but the level still remains five times higher than in more industrially developed countries such as Germany. The health of the populations in different Mexican states, however, varies dramatically. For example, the state of Oaxaca has the highest infant mortality rate in Mexico, with 42 deaths per 1,000 live births in 2000, whereas Quintana Roo and Nuevo León had just 18 and 17 deaths per 1,000 births respectively in the same year. These differences are also evident in the context of other indicators of development. States such as Guerrero, Oaxaca and Chiapas are among the poorest in Mexico. The people living there have a lower life expectancy than the national average, and families tend to be larger.

The Mexican government has made great efforts to improve the health of the population over the last few years through a variety of health initiatives. Among such initiatives were several highly successful vaccination programs to reduce the incidence of whooping cough, tuberculosis and polio. The government continues to try to prevent outbreaks of these diseases and also to control the spread of killer diseases such as cholera and HIV/AIDS.

For such a wealthy country, Mexico has a very high level of malnutrition. In an effort to improve this situation the Mexican government has begun a number of food support programs. In 2000, 4 million children received free milk, 3 million children received free school breakfasts and a further 1 million families received 1kg per day of tortillas. Despite these efforts, the gap between the rich and poor in Mexico is still huge.

Students collect money on behalf of the Red Cross, an emergency service that is free to all.

This man does not have access to piped water. He draws his water from a communal well.

inside the house and nearly 30 percent had only outside access. The remaining 5 percent used public hydrants or collected water from other people's homes.

There is also a large difference in access to basic services between urban and rural areas. In towns and cities with populations of more than 100,000 people, almost every household had access to electricity and water in 2000. However, in localities with populations of 2,500 and below, the proportion of people with access to electricity and water was significantly lower. In one of the poorest states, Oaxaca, only 38 percent of all homes had a combination of access to water in the home, to a drainage system and to electricity.

BASIC SERVICES

Over the last 30 years there has been a significant improvement in the provision of essential services such as clean water, cooking gas, electricity and drainage to Mexican homes. In 1970 more than a third of homes had no access to water or electricity. By 2000, 95 percent of all homes had access to electricity and 85 percent had water piped to their homes. Similarly, less than half of all homes in Mexico had access to drainage in 1970, but by 2000, 78 percent of all homes were linked to the main drainage system.

While these figures appear to show vast improvements to the provision of basic services, a closer look shows that Mexico is still a long way behind the developed nations. For example, while 85 percent of the population have water piped to their homes, less than 16 percent of these people were connected to water mains and the remaining 84 percent had untreated water piped to their homes directly from rivers, lakes or wells. Only 65 percent of homes actually had water

An old woman in a rural area of Michoacán state collects firewood for cooking and heating.

Most people in Mexico now cook using gas. However, nearly a fifth of the population still use firewood or charcoal for fuel. In 2000, 98 percent of the population in Mexico City used gas for cooking fuel, while more than half of the homes in Oaxaca used firewood or charcoal.

THE MEXICAN DIET

Mexican food is still largely based on the pre-Hispanic traditional staple foods of beans, corn (maize) and chilies. Maize is typically ground into flour and served as flat pancakes called tortillas. An average Mexican eats more than 1kg of tortillas every day. Tortillas are eaten as an accompaniment to almost every meal. The diet of millions of Mexicans consists almost entirely of tortillas, beans and chilies, supplemented with small amounts of meat and local fruits. This diet is very well balanced in terms of vitamins, minerals, carbohydrates and protein, and Mexico has fewer problems with obesity than many Western nations.

The discovery of Mexico led to the introduction of many foods such as maize, chocolate, vanilla, chilies, peanuts and avocados to the rest of the world. At the same time the Spanish colonizers also introduced many European staple foods, such as wheat, rice, vegetables and beef cattle, which have been incorporated into the modern Mexican diet.

Over the last 30 years the average Mexican diet has improved dramatically. However, there is a marked difference between the diets of rich and poor people and the diets of those who live in urban and rural areas. According to the World Health Organization, around 40 percent of Mexicans are suffering from malnutrition.

Even small stores have a machine to make as many tortillas as possible.

MEXICAN FAST FOOD

The smell of delicious food being prepared fills the streets of towns and cities throughout Mexico. At the roadside, small food stalls serve a variety of traditional "fast foods" served in tortillas rather than on plates. Tacos, for example, are a popular snack made with beans, meat, chilies and tomatoes wrapped in a fried tortilla. Enchiladas are also popular and consist of a meat or bean filling covered in cheese and a spicy sauce.

RELIGION

In 1521 the Spanish *conquistadores* introduced Christianity to Mexico in the form of Roman Catholicism. Festivals throughout the year celebrate saints' days and all the major Christian events. In the census of 2000, 88 percent of Mexico's population were Catholic. However, millions of Mexicans still observe many pre-Hispanic traditions. Throughout the country colorful costumes, traditional crafts and ceremonial events that predate the arrival of the Spanish can be seen. Many indigenous religious festivals coincide with those of the Christian calendar, for example the Day of the Dead and All Saints' Day.

People in Angangueo, Michoacán, take part in a Catholic festival to celebrate their patron saint.

CASE STUDY
DAY OF THE DEAD

Families spend all night in the cemeteries, remembering their deceased relatives.

The festival of *Dia de Muertos*, or Day of the Dead, is a tradition that dates back to well before the first Europeans arrived in Mexico. It is based on the belief of the Tarascan people, an indigenous group that lives around Lake Pátzcuaro, that once a year the souls of the dead return to visit their loved ones.

Many pre-Hispanic celebrations disappeared after the introduction of Christianity. However, *Dia de Muertos* coincided with two important days in the Roman Catholic calendar – All Saints' Day and All Souls' Day. These Christian celebrations shared much with the pagan *Dia de Muertos*, including the laying of flowers at family graves, the burning of candles and offerings of food. The celebrations combined over the centuries to form the celebration that takes place in Mexico today. Generally, families spend one or two nights between 31 October and 2 November in the graveyards, remembering their loved ones. Across Mexico the Day of the Dead celebrations have borrowed influences from other cultures, such as the Aztec death god, Mictlantecutli, who is often represented as skull motifs in food and candles, and more recently elements of Halloween from the United States.

EDUCATION

In the last 10 years the Mexican government has made the improvement of the national education system a priority, and today around 5 percent of Mexico's GDP is spent on education. Primary education is free and compulsory for children between the ages of five and 11. However, education records show that only around six out of 10 primary school children complete their schooling. Between 1992 and 1998, the government made secondary education compulsory in an effort to increase the numbers of students who complete their studies and then go on to higher education. However, Mexico has a very poor higher education record. During 2000–01 only 1,860 students per 100,000 had gone on to higher education, compared with 5,500 students per 100,000 in the United States.

There is a major divide in the availability and quality of education between urban and rural locations. While basic primary schooling is available to virtually everyone, urban schools tend to have better facilities and have smaller class sizes than those in rural areas. Secondary schooling is not available in many remote areas and parents have to consider sending their children away from the village, sometimes as boarding students. Despite the government's attempts to improve the situation, in 2000 almost 10 percent of the

Teaching computer skills is a high priority in Mexican schools.

population over the age of 15 was illiterate and only 70 percent of people in this age group had completed their primary education. The percentage of the population aged 15 and over that had completed their secondary education was 46 percent.

Students walk through the grounds of Mexico City's university on their way to lectures.

UNIVERSITY

The *Universidad Nacional Autonoma de Mexico* (UNAM), situated in Mexico City, is the largest and oldest university in the Americas. It was founded in 1551 and today has more than 270,000 students and 30,000 lecturers. Most of the main buildings date from the 1950s, and many of them are covered in murals by famous artists. The university is so large that students take buses and taxis to get from one department to another.

FAMILY LIFE

Family ties in Mexico are traditionally very strong. It is quite usual for members of several generations to live together as one large extended family group. On holidays and special occasions such as birthdays it is typical for children, parents, uncles and aunts, and grandparents to celebrate together. This style of living is essential in homes where both parents have to work full time, since grandparents can care for the younger family members. However, the difficulty of daily life, especially in rural areas, is leading to a breakdown in this traditional family model. More people are leaving their home villages and towns in search of better-paid work in other parts of the country. In remote rural villages it is common to find that most of the young people have left and that only the elderly remain.

ROLES OF WOMEN

The role of women in Mexican society has also changed over the last 50 years. Young women today expect to work, stay single longer, marry later and have fewer children than women of their mothers' generation. Women often have to balance the responsibilities of work and caring for a family. The change in the role of women has come about mainly because most people now live in urban areas, where access to education and work for women is much better than in the countryside.

The number of women working in Mexico has risen steadily over the last 20 years. This woman works in a timber mill.

FEMALE LABOR FORCE (% OF TOTAL)

Source: Social Watch (February 2003)

RECREATION

Mexican people love a fiesta (a big celebration), and throughout the year there are numerous opportunities for these. Saints' days and public holidays are all celebrated with music and dancing. On Saturday nights in Mexico City one street is full of mariachi musicians, small bands who play traditional Mexican music and are hired for parties. Family occasions such as birthdays, baptisms and marriages are also particularly important to the typical Mexican family, and they are usually accompanied by lively celebrations.

Mexican people also love sports. On Sundays the parks are crowded with people playing soccer or basketball or just jogging. Of all the sports, soccer is the most popular. Mexico City is home to the huge Azteca Stadium. Basketball has grown in popularity over the last 20 years. There are also some regional variations in sports – rodeos are popular in many northern states, while the beautiful coastal waters in the south attract snorkelers, windsurfers and sunbathers.

TELEVISION OWNERSHIP

Television sets per thousand people

300
270
240
210
180
150
120
90
60
30

1970 1975 1980 1985 1990 1995 2000

Source: International Telecommunications Union

THE GIANT STADIUMS OF MEXICO CITY

The Azteca soccer stadium is one of the largest in the world. Home to the first-division team América, it can hold more than 100,000 flag-waving fans when full. The biggest match of the season is when América plays Guadalajara.

The Olympic Stadium, built for the 1968 Olympics, is only slightly smaller and holds around 80,000 people.

Like most countries that were once colonies of Spain, Mexico still has competitive bullfighting. On weekends between October and March spectators flock to see bullfights in the Monumental Plaza Mexico, a huge concrete bowl that can hold up to 48,000 people.

Azteca Stadium is filled to capacity for a cup final match.

MEXICO'S ECONOMY

In Veracruz state bananas and oranges are grown intensively for export.

Until the Second World War Mexico was mostly an agricultural society. However, in the last 50 years the country has undergone a dramatic change. Mexico is now a highly industrialized nation, an economically developed country and one of the 20 wealthiest countries in the world. Manufacturing and oil production provide the backbone to Mexico's economy, but services such as tourism are the most important in terms of the number of jobs they provide.

Today, Mexico's economy can be divided into three main sections – industrial production, agricultural production and services. Industrial and agricultural production include the parts of the economy where products are manufactured, cultivated or mined. Services are activities that are paid for although no actual goods are produced, such as tourism and banking.

AGRICULTURE AND FISHING

Although the importance of agriculture to the Mexican economy has been reducing since the Second World War, Mexican crop production is still among the highest in the world, and Mexico remains a major agricultural producer. Agriculture generates 5 percent of Mexico's GDP and employs 23 percent of the country's workforce. While some areas of Mexico use the

FARMING AREAS

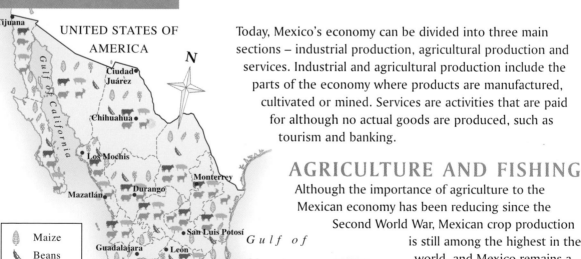

N

Legend:
- Maize
- Beans
- Wheat
- Sorghum
- Cattle
- Sheep
- Pigs
- Goats

UNITED STATES OF AMERICA

Tijuana
Ciudad Juárez
Chihuahua
Los Mochis
Monterrey
Durango
Mazatlán
San Luis Potosí
Guadalajara
León
Mexico City
Puebla
Veracruz
Acapulco
Oaxaca
Mérida
Cancún

Gulf of California

Gulf of Mexico

BELIZE
GUATEMALA
HONDURAS
EL SALVADOR

0   500km
0   300 miles

latest techniques to grow commercial crops, more than half of Mexico's land is owned as small family or communal farms, which produce mainly food and products for local consumption. The main crops grown for export are coffee, sugar, fruits and vegetables (accounting for 3–4 percent of all exports), while maize, beans, wheat and sorghum are produced for consumption within Mexico.

Production of a number of major crops has been decreasing for many years. For example, sugarcane production fell by nearly 3 million tonnes between 1998 and 1999 to 47 million tonnes. Mexico now imports maize, the staple food, in order to supplement its fast-reducing national harvest, which decreased from about 18 million tonnes in 1995 to 16 million tonnes in 1999. Livestock production has remained fairly constant over the last decade with milk, eggs and poultry all showing yearly rises. In Mexico 30 percent of agriculture is made up of livestock farms, the majority of which raise cattle and poultry. In 1999, 4 million tonnes of meat and a record 9 billion liters of milk were produced.

While most Mexican agricultural output is declining, some areas are expanding. The fastest growing and most productive agricultural area today is the northern desert in states such as Chihuahua, Sonora and Sinaloa. Here large farms have been set up using irrigation systems to grow everything from cotton to chili peppers.

The amount of land used to grow arable (cereal) crops, such as wheat and soybean, has been expanded through the irrigation of arid areas. While small-scale subsistence agriculture remains widespread, new intensive farming methods are being employed to increase the productivity of the land.

Tomatoes are grown on irrigated land in the Sonoran Desert, near Los Mochis.

Given the country's long coastline, some economists suggest that Mexico is not realizing the full potential of its fish stocks. In 2000 the national catch was 1.4 million tonnes. The main types of fish caught were tuna, shrimp, sardine and squid. The national fishing fleet consists of about 100,000 fishing boats. The fish catch more than satisfies the national demand of just 11.1kg of fish per person per year. Much of the valuable catch is exported. In 2000 the export earnings of fish totaled US$679 million.

Along the Yucatán coast are small fleets of octopus fishing boats.

MANUFACTURING

The manufacturing sector is the most important part of the Mexican economy in terms of exports and foreign income. It was originally set up after the Second World War as a way to reduce Mexico's dependence on imports. However, this sector is now mainly involved in earning foreign income to help repay the country's huge international debt. Since the end of the Second World War in 1945, exports of manufactured goods, including metal products, machinery and chemical products such as plastics and medicines, have risen from 24 percent of all exports to 88 percent of Mexico's exports in 2000.

MAQUILADORAS

Mexico's fastest-growing industries are the maquiladora industries. Maquiladoras are basically in-bond assembly plants – factories in Mexico that are involved in the assembly of a wide range of brand-name goods under license for foreign companies. The companies, mostly American or Japanese, have their goods such as cars, jeans and televisions made in Mexico because labor costs are much lower there than in the United States or Japan. The majority of goods produced are exported to the United States.

Modern maquiladora factories like this one in Chihuahua are becoming an increasingly common sight in the northern cities of Mexico.

LATIN AMERICAN DEBT CRISIS

In 1982 Mexico caused what is known as the Latin American Debt Crisis. This was when Mexico refused to pay the interest on its loans from wealthier countries. The result was that loans for the building of roads, dams, and factories, for example, were stopped, and Mexico was forced to alter its economy to pay back the money. This situation drastically changed the Mexican economy. Not only did the wealth of Mexicans decline sharply, but the manufacturing industries turned their attention to the more lucrative business of producing goods for export in an effort to increase foreign income to help pay the interest on the loans.

The interest on Mexico's vast loans is still the country's largest single payment every year. In the last five years this annual payment has ranged from US$12 billion and US$13.5 billion.

THE INFORMAL SECTOR

In 2000 the National Institute of Statistics, Geography and Informatics (INEGI), a government department, carried out a survey to measure the size of Mexico's informal sector. People in this sector work off the record, for cash, and not as registered members of the workforce. This means they do not pay tax on their earnings, but they have no employment rights. The figures revealed that, excluding illegal activities such as drug trafficking, the informal sector had a value of US$47 billion, equivalent to nearly 13 percent of Mexico's GDP. Shops and restaurants employed the most people who were not paying tax and had no employment rights, with about 31 percent of all workers falling into the informal category.

Street vendors, who pay no tax, make up a large part of Mexico's informal sector.

Further opportunities to expand the maquiladora industry have arisen from a new free trade agreement between Mexico and the European Union in March 2000. This means that Mexican goods can be more easily traded with European countries because the additional taxes that were once put on Mexican produce (making them more expensive in Europe) have now been mostly removed. For instance, the city of Mérida in the Yucatán Peninsula already has a thriving export economy due to its ideal location for trade with Europe. It is estimated that the city's contribution to the total maquiladora export will double between 2000 and 2005 from 0.7 percent to beyond 1.5 percent.

The success of the maquiladora industry in the last 20 years has led to the rapid economic development of cities close to the US border, such as Chihuahua, Tijuana, Ciudad Juárez and Monterrey. In 1999 more than 50 percent of all industrial exports were from maquiladora factories, generating a massive US$63,748,000 in export revenue. The growth of the maquiladora industry has been dramatic. In 1996 there were 3,047 maquiladora plants in Mexico employing 815,000 people. Today there are 3,667 maquiladora plants in Mexico, employing nearly 1.3 million people.

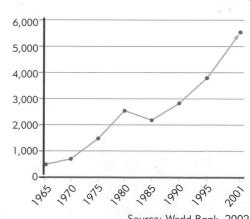

GNI (GROSS NATIONAL INCOME) PER CAPITA (US$)

Source: World Bank, 2002

EXPORTS AND TRADE

Mexico's economy is dominated by its relationship with the United States. In 2000 the United States was the final destination for the majority of all Mexican exports. A new trade agreement between Mexico and Europe is likely to alter the percentage of exports slightly, but the United States will be Mexico's main trading partner well into the twenty-first century. Mexico has special access to US and Canadian markets as part of the North America Free Trade Agreement (NAFTA), which came into effect in 1994. However, overdependence on the United States and the limited number of export products made means that Mexico's exports are vulnerable if there is a change in US economic fortunes.

The Mexican economy has undergone a major transformation in the last 20 years. One of the main changes is the way that Mexico has developed its export industries.

Veracruz is one of Mexico's largest ports, handling huge volumes of agricultural and manufactured exports every year.

MAJOR TRADING PARTNERS % GDP 2001

EXPORTS

Netherlands Antilles 0.6%
UK 0.4%
Spain 0.8%
Germany 0.9%
Canada 2%
Other 6.9%
US 88.4%

IMPORTS

Italy 1.3%
Brazil 1.1%
Taiwan 1.6%
S. Korea 2.1%
China 2.2%
Canada 2.5%
Germany 3.6%
Japan 4.7%
Other 12.5%
US 68.4%

Source: *CIA World Factbook*, 2002

For example, in 1980 the largest single export was crude petroleum, which accounted for 61 percent of all exports. At this time the export income from oil was supported by other products such as gas, cotton, coffee, silver and copper, which when combined made up a further 12.4 percent of exports.

By 2000 crude petroleum accounted for only 10 percent of all exports. By 2002, the combined income from all exports of manufactured goods had risen to 91 percent. This was mainly due to the development of maquiladora factories (see page 40). Imports have also changed, and 77 percent of all imports in 1999 were materials to be used in the maquiladora industries.

CASE STUDY
OIL

In 2000, Mexico produced an annual average of 3.5 million barrels of crude oil or liquid gas equivalent. Oil sales both internationally and nationally are very important for raising government income in the form of taxes. In 2000 oil-related income accounted for more than a third of all government revenue.

Mexican oil production and distribution is monopolized by the state-owned company Petroleros Mexicanos (PEMEX), which is one of the world's largest oil companies. However, many analysts state that the company is overstaffed, never operates at full capacity, is a source of political donations and is open to corruption. Because of its inefficiency there are plans to privatize PEMEX.

CASE STUDY
VANILLA

All vanilla flowers on plantations have to be pollinated by hand.

The vanilla plant is a type of orchid. In the wild it grows up the trunks of rain forest trees. On commercial plantations orchids can grow up many species of tree, including orange trees.

Vanilla is native to Mexico, but today it is grown throughout the world. Mexico is the world's fourth-largest producer of vanilla pods, with a harvest of 299 tonnes in 2001. Vanilla is grown primarily in the state of Veracruz. Mexican vanilla is considered to be the best in the world in terms of flavor and aroma. It is Mexico's most valuable crop in terms of income per hectare.

To produce vanilla pods, the flowers of the orchid need to be pollinated. This sounds easy, but each orchid flower is only open for five hours each year. Therefore, in the flowering season teams of workers inspect the flowers in plantations every morning and pollinate any open flower before midday to ensure a good crop.

THE SERVICE INDUSTRY

The growth of the service sector of a country is tied to its economic development. In the last 50 years Mexico has transformed itself from a primarily agricultural and mining society into a modern industrial economy characterized by a large service sector.

The service industry includes banking, computer programming, tourism and catering, as well as public services (such as health services). The service industry is the most important part of the Mexican economy in terms of employment. It has grown significantly over the last 20 years and in 2001 services accounted for 69 percent of GDP.

Tourism is one of Mexico's most valuable service industries, growing steadily over the last 20 years. In 1999 more than 10 million foreign tourists visited Mexico, generating US$5.4 billion, and US day-trippers spent a further US$444 million. Mexico's tourist industry employs about 2 million people, and the numbers are increasing as this sector continues to grow. Mexico's spectacular natural attractions such as its reefs on the Caribbean coast, the monarch butterfly winter gathering sites in Michoacán state and rare whale species in the Gulf of California are also attracting tourists from all over the world.

ECONOMIC STRUCTURE GDP

- Agriculture 5%
- Industry 26%
- Services 69%

Source: CIA World Factbook, 2002

Tourists like these visitors to Copper Canyon provide valuable foreign income to Mexico.

Cancún was once just a small fishing village on the Caribbean coast, in the state of Quintana Roo. In the1970s the government decided to create a brand-new tourist resort in the south of Mexico to rival Acapulco, one of Mexico's most popular Pacific coast resorts. The goal was to produce a tourist facility to take advantage of the blue Caribbean waters with their coral reefs, the golden sand and the constant tropical temperature. During the 1980s the infrastructure required to support a major tourist area was built. This included highways, an international airport, electricity supply, and water and sewage systems. Today, Cancún's main hotel area is on a narrow island that is 15km long. Cancún is hugely successful, catering mainly to US tourists and creating a popular tourist resort, where more than 2 million people come to visit each year.

White, sandy beaches and the tropical Caribbean Sea attract millions of tourists to Cancún each year.

TRANSPORT AND COMMUNICATIONS

Mexico has an excellent network of roads and railways linking the country's main economic areas. However, there are numerous barriers to movement in Mexico such as the Western and Eastern Sierra Madre mountain ranges.

In 2000 Mexico had 331,635km of roads, of which only one third were paved. In addition, the railways, which have been declining in importance as a means of transporting people and goods over the last 30 years, have a total of 26,622km of track. Mexico has an excellent network of 29 domestic airports throughout the country and the total number of air passengers for the year 2000 was just over 3 million. While many of the exports leave the country by truck, Mexico has 108 ports of varying importance for exporting oil and other cargoes.

TRANSPORT

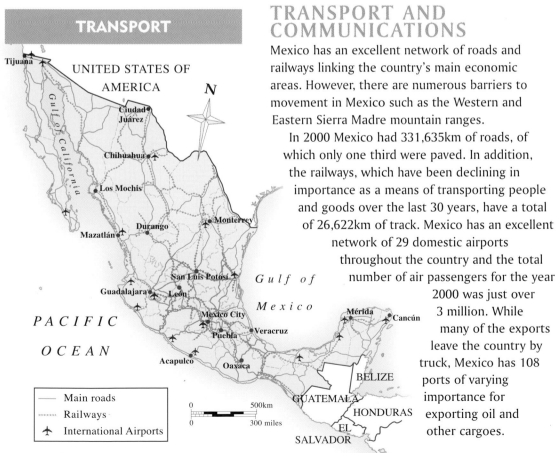

Main roads
Railways
International Airports

0   500km
0   300 miles

THE ENVIRONMENT

Giant organ-pipe cacti are a familiar sight in the Sonoran Desert.

Mexico has many different types of natural environments. These include North America's largest desert, rugged mountain ranges with alpine and tropical vegetation, tropical mangrove-lined beaches and part of Central America's largest remaining tract of rain forest. However, this diversity is under threat. Much of Mexico is suffering environmental problems including deforestation, conversion of land to agriculture, and serious air and water pollution.

MEXICO'S BIODIVERSITY

Biodiversity is just a short way of saying biological diversity, which means the variety of different species of plants and animals. Mexico has an extremely varied landscape and a huge diversity of habitats. A quarter of all reptile species and 10 percent of all mammal, bird, and fish species on the planet are found in Mexico. There are 30 percent more bird species than in the United States and Canada combined. Mexico is also very important to migrating wildlife since it acts as a corridor between South and North America. The most famous migration is that of the monarch butterflies.

NUMBERS OF SPECIES

Mammals	450	(69)
Birds	769	(39)
Plants	26,071	(1,593)

(Endangered species in parentheses)

Source: World Development Indicators, 2002

DESERT HABITATS

More than half of Mexico is desert or semi-desert. The two largest deserts are the Chihuahua Desert and Sonoran Desert, which occupy most of the north of the country. The deserts are home to many types of wildlife, including black bears, pumas, pronghorns (North America's only antelope), 13 species of rattlesnake, and many types of birds. The Chihuahua and Sonoran Deserts are particularly important habitats for rare plants such as the peyote cactus, Chihuahua's own subspecies of wolf and over 100 species of fish. However, large areas of desert are being destroyed by the overgrazing of cattle and horses, conversion to irrigated agricultural land and overextraction of water.

Water is a scarce resource in the Chihuahua and Sonoran Deserts, but every day millions of gallons are extracted from the few major rivers and used for agriculture and human consumption. Agriculture is by far the largest user of water resources in Mexico, accounting for 78 percent of all fresh water use. The deserts are becoming drier and the important wetlands at the heart of the Chihuahua Desert are in danger of disappearing along with their unique wildlife.

The growth in the industrial cities close to the US border has led to serious water pollution, particularly in the two main northern rivers of Rio Conchos and Rio Grande (also called Rio Bravo). Pollution, intensive agriculture, and the expanding urban areas are all having a serious effect on the desert wildlife.

CASE STUDY
MONARCH BUTTERFLY RESERVES

In 2003 one of the colonies of monarch butterflies in Michoacán state was estimated to be made up of over 1 billion individuals.

Every year, millions of monarch butterflies migrate from Canada and the United States to a small area of pine forest in central Mexico. Arriving at the beginning of November, these butterflies cling to native pine trees in huge numbers. Often whole trees are covered so that they appear brown rather than green. Sometimes the weight on the trees is so great that branches snap off.

In 1986 the government decreed that the Monarch Butterfly Reserve covering 16,000 hectares was to be protected. However, studies in the 1990s showed that the forest was still being cut down and that 44 percent had been degraded. To prevent the situation from getting worse, in 2000 the Monarch Butterfly Reserve was extended to cover 56,000 hectares. The World Wide Fund for Nature (WWF) and the Mexican Fund for Conservation of Nature set up a scheme whereby people in the area could claim compensation for not cutting down the trees in the reserve.

COASTAL ENVIRONMENTS

Mexico has some of the most spectacular beaches and coastal waters in the world. In the south, tropical beaches face the turquoise waters of the Caribbean Sea with its reefs and spectacular marine wildlife. In the north the Gulf of California has the highest concentration of cetacean (whale and dolphin) species anywhere in the world.

The Gulf of California is enclosed on three sides by Baja California and the northwestern states of Sinaloa and Sonora. Throughout the year 13 species of whale, dolphin, and porpoise can be observed there. The Gulf of California is also home to the world's rarest porpoise, the vaquita, the population of which is believed to be less than 20. Despite the importance of conservation in this area, the Gulf is undergoing serious change. Complex chemicals used in Mexican and US agriculture are finding their way into its waters, causing irreversible poisoning to many species.

A jaguar rests during the day in the shade of a forest.

The beautiful Pacific coastline and Yucatán Peninsula are major tourist attractions. Huge hotel complexes have sprung up in places like Cancún. But action will be needed to protect the natural beauty of the area. Mangrove forests are breeding grounds for many fish, and wetlands provide homes for manatees and giant turtles. Yet these areas are under threat from the uncontrolled expansion of many tourist resorts.

MEXICAN FORESTS

In 2000 Mexico's forests extended over 552,000km^2 – about 29 percent of the country's land area. These forests range from the dense tropical rain forest in the south to extensive pine forests that cover much of Mexico's mountainous terrain. Mexico has a large number of tree species, and it has more pine and oak tree species than any other country in the world.

In the far south, Mexico has areas of spectacular rain forest that contain jaguars, hummingbirds and many more rare and beautiful creatures. These forests are under threat from expanding agricultural areas such

as coffee plantations and cattle ranches. Mexico's rain forest forms part of El Peten – the largest continuous area of rain forest in Central America. El Peten is a refuge for some of Central America's rarest wildlife. A number of conservation projects have been started, such as setting up community-based forest management schemes for the extraction of small volumes of timber and forest products. The largest undisturbed area of mature rain forest is the Lacondon Forest in the state of Chiapas.

Mexico also has huge areas of temperate forest, many of which are dominated by pine and oak species. Even in the dry northern part of the country the desert gives way to forest on the higher ground. In central Mexico, where the rainfall is higher, there were once dense mixed forests of pine and oak. However, the native Mexican temperate forests have been exploited for centuries. Today much of the original forest has disappeared. Demand for firewood in rural areas and timber for pulp and paper has been the main cause of deforestation. Every year more than 6,300km² of forest are destroyed.

An area of forest has been burned to make way for agriculture in the state of Oaxaca.

IGUANA PROJECT

In the tropical forests of southern Mexico many people hunt iguanas. These tree-living reptiles can grow to over 1m long and feature in the diets of many rain forest people. In some areas of tropical forest the iguanas have been overhunted and the populations have been significantly reduced. However, a number of new community-based projects have been started up to collect iguana eggs. The eggs are hatched and the iguanas are fed until they are big enough to defend themselves. Then they are released into the wild to breed.

This young iguana is about to be released.

URBAN POLLUTION

Most urban populations in Mexico are exposed to serious health risks from polluted air. Mexico City is one of the most polluted cities in the world. A dense, brown smog of unhealthy gases hangs over the city most days of the year. The smog contains a cocktail of pollutants such as carbon monoxide, lead and complex toxic compounds. Every day 12,000 tonnes of pollutants are added to the smog. Inhabitants of Mexico City have over twice the level of lead in their blood as do residents of other major cities around the world. Smog hangs over most large Mexican cities including Tijuana, Chihuahua, Ciudad Juárez, Oaxaca and Mérida.

In urban areas, water pollution is also a major environmental problem. In the northern city of Ciudad Juárez, for example, the Rio Grande is the main source of water and the main sewer. In Mexico City the Panuco River receives 690,000 tonnes of untreated sewage every year.

Many Mexican waterways are contaminated with industrial and household waste.

The problems are particularly serious in the north of the country, where there are few major rivers and inadequate rainfall.

CASE STUDY
WATER USE AND ABUSE

WATER POLLUTION BY ORIGIN

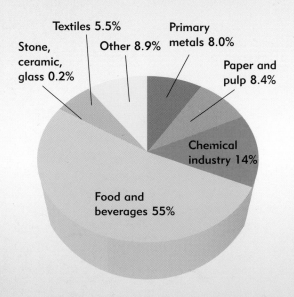

Textiles 5.5%

Other 8.9%

Primary metals 8.0%

Stone, ceramic, glass 0.2%

Paper and pulp 8.4%

Chemical industry 14%

Food and beverages 55%

Source: World Development Indicators, 1999

Water is one of Mexico's most critical resources. Every year 70 billion to 80 billion cubic meters of water are extracted from Mexico's rivers, lakes, and underground reservoirs. More than 78 percent of this water is used to irrigate crops and 5 percent is used in industry. The remaining 17 percent of water extracted is used by Mexico's population in their homes and gardens. In desert regions, much of the water used is extracted from underground reservoirs, called aquifers. However, the demand for water is so great that these underground reservoirs are rapidly becoming exhausted. For example, it is calculated that the underground water source that serves Ciudad Juárez will run dry by 2025 if water conservation measures are not taken soon. The situation in Mexico is very serious because more than half the country has low levels of rainfall (less than 500mm a year) and more than three quarters of the population live in these arid zones.

The levels of polluting gases such as nitrogen dioxide, ozone and sulfur dioxide in Mexico City are more than double those found in Tokyo and New York. Most of the pollution comes from the estimated 5 million vehicles in the city and the heavy industry in the suburbs. The situation is made worse because Mexico City is at the center of a natural bowl shape that is ringed by high mountains. This prevents pollutants in the air from dispersing easily. The situation is so bad that the newspapers publish pollution forecasts so that people with respiratory problems can leave the city or seek medical help if necessary. When pollutants rise to extremely dangerous levels, Mexico City's Environmental Contingency Plan comes in to operation. This starts with "Double No Drive Day," which restricts the number of cars on the roads. If high pollution levels persist for three days or more, industrial activity is reduced.

TOP: Air pollution in Mexico City can be so bad that it is possible to see only a few blocks away.
ABOVE: Heavy traffic is the main source of Mexico City's pollution problem.

In extreme emergencies all traffic and industry are halted, and only emergency vehicles are permitted on the streets.

RURAL PROBLEMS

Rural areas of Mexico face many environmental problems. Agricultural production has a major environmental impact on these areas. For example, soil erosion is particularly serious in Mexico because many crops are cultivated on steep land or on light soils that can be easily washed away by rain or blown away by wind. On the huge mechanized farms of the north and central Mexico few measures are taken to stop tons of soil being blown away by the wind each year. Overgrazing these areas strips away the plant cover that helps bind the soil. This leads to great dust storms as the topsoil is blown away.

Much of Mexico's most productive agricultural land is in arid regions. These areas require irrigation to produce crops such as cotton, chili peppers and pecan nuts. Irrigation leads to overuse of precious water resources and also causes a process known as salination, where salt builds up on the soil surface and contaminates watercourses such as natural streams.

Soil erosion and desertification are becoming increasingly serious problems in Mexico.

The use of pesticides and herbicides, especially on crops such as cotton, reduces biodiversity around the agricultural areas, killing not only pests but also many other types of insects and plants.

In rural locations, natural forest and other habitats are being destroyed by local people. The unequal division of land between rich and poor forces many people to move into wild areas to grow crops, collect food or hunt wild animals. Rural people often do

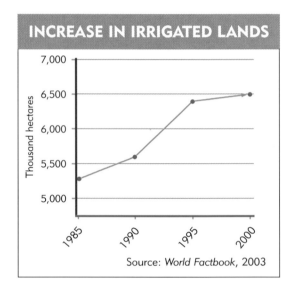

INCREASE IN IRRIGATED LANDS

Source: *World Factbook*, 2003

Many communities are trying to reverse deforestation by planting tree seedlings in their forest areas.

not have access to electricity and gas, so many of them heat their homes and cook using firewood collected from the forests. This is a major cause of deforestation. Habitat destruction is one of the main factors causing many Mexican species to become endangered.

POSITIVE SOLUTIONS

Many Mexicans and Mexican organizations are working hard to reduce the impact of people on the environment. The government has created 66,400km² of protected areas, accounting for 3.5 percent of the entire country's land area. However, the departments responsible for policing and managing these areas are not given sufficient resources to do so. To make young people more aware of the environmental problems facing the country, curricula in both primary and secondary schools now include environmental education. The government has implemented many measures to reduce urban pollution. These include providing cheap, efficient public transport so that people will leave their cars at home and restricting the

numbers of days that older cars with higher pollution levels are allowed on the roads. However, the huge scale of Mexico's environmental problems means that such programs have had only limited success.

In addition to the government's efforts, numerous communities and nongovernmental organizations (NGOs) such the WWF are campaigning to reduce harmful impacts on Mexico's natural resources. They are also working to maintain rare habitats in an effort to prevent the extinction of some of Mexico's spectacular and rare species such as the Chihuahuan wolf, quetzal (a type of bird) and gila monster (a type of lizard). Indigenous groups of people such as the Zapotec Indians in Oaxaca have also been fiercely defending their traditional lands from exploitation by outsiders. The Zapotec Indians and many other communities around Mexico are developing ecotourism schemes as a way of earning money while protecting natural habitats.

LOOKING AHEAD

A view of the financial center of Mexico City hints at Mexico's hidden wealth.

Mexico is a country of spectacular natural wealth. It is rich in commodities that are in demand all over the world. For example, Mexico is the world's largest producer of silver, and it has significant deposits of other key metals and minerals, such as copper, aluminum and zinc. At the same time, Mexico has vast deposits of vital fossil fuels in the form of coal, gas and particularly oil. This guarantees energy supplies for at least 50 years and enables the country to avoid importing oil, something that compromises many economies around the world.

ECONOMIC POTENTIAL

The economic potential of Mexico is enormous. Rich in natural resources, Mexico also has a relatively young population and hence a large energetic workforce. This is particularly clear in comparison with countries such as Germany and the United Kingdom that now have ageing populations. In addition Mexico is fortunate to border the United States, a nation of high consumers creating a huge demand for cheaply produced goods. However, Mexico's dependence on trade with the United States also makes the country vulnerable. A downturn in the US economy, such as the one that happened after the World Trade Center was attacked on 11 September 2001, has immediate repercussions on Mexico's economy.

ADDRESSING THE RICH-POOR DIVIDE

One of the striking things about life in Mexico is the huge gap between the lifestyles of the rich and poor. In Zona Rosa in Mexico City, for example, people in the streets appear to be very affluent – wearing designer clothes, talking into mobile phones and driving around in expensive imported cars. In fact the scene is not unlike many European cities. In contrast, just a few miles away are sprawling slums housing some of the millions of people recognized by the World Health Organization as living below the poverty line. Temporary shacks without access to electricity or clean drinking water house families who represent Mexico's urban poor. But this vast gap exists not only in Mexico City. There are also sharp divisions in the quality of life of people from different states and regions and between towns and countryside. Further divisions exist between ethnic groups. Many of Mexico's 10 million indigenous people are among the poorest people in the country, while the European minority enjoys a significantly higher standard of living.

Mexico needs to address the huge inequalities that exist in its society before it can begin to realize its full potential. Corruption in politics and in many parts of the economy leads to the production of a new batch of billionaires at the end of each government term of office; at the same time the economy remains in a state of ruin, despite the nation's obvious wealth.

Unlike many developing nations, which lack key resources or occupy an isolated location in the world, Mexico has a powerful economy based on a wealth of natural resources, with access to the huge US market. Despite such resources, lack of political will, large-scale corruption and the repayment of huge foreign debts are hampering the further development of Mexico.

Many Mexican families remain malnourished and lack basic services in the twenty-first century.

TELECOMMUNICATIONS DATA

Mainline Phones	12,332,000
Mobile Phones	2,020,000
Internet Service Providers	51

Source: *CIA World Factbook*, 2002
*Latest figures are 1998

PERSONAL COMPUTERS

Computers (per 1,000 people)

60
50
40
30
20
10
0

1990 1992 1994 1996 1998 2000

Sources: World Development Indicators, World Bank, 2002

ENVIRONMENTAL CHALLENGES

Each year, thousands of tourists pay to go whale watching off the coast of Mexico. These magnificent creatures are now protected.

Despite Mexico's huge economic potential the nation could suffer greatly if many of its serious environmental problems are not tackled. For example, the quality of the air is so poor in Mexico City that millions of people are at risk of serious health problems. Air pollution may have a domino effect, leading to a reduction in productivity in the city as more people have to take time off work due to illness. Health problems also present a huge cost to the governmental resources such as health services. The same domino effect may be triggered by Mexico's water pollution problem. Many of Mexico's waterways are contaminated with millions of gallons of untreated sewage every day and pose a serious risk to the health of people who have to use the water.

The overuse of water resources, both above and below ground, will lead to great problems if nothing is done. More than half of the country is arid and in danger of running out of water in the next 50 years. Added to this is the problem of global warming, which could speed up desertification in the north and lead to even more violent weather conditions in the south.

Mexico is a country of spectacular beauty. Dramatic volcanoes, rugged mountain ranges, tropical beaches, and a huge variety of habitats for wildlife all exist within its borders. This natural beauty attracts millions of tourists, who spend billions of dollars each year. The tourist industry also provides hundreds of thousands of jobs for Mexican people. Another part of Mexico's natural wealth is its remarkable biodiversity. The country has at least 10 percent of all species of birds, plants and mammals on the planet. The conservation of rare species such as whales and the preservation of many of the spectacularly beautiful areas of landscape are vital not only for nature but also to maintain the tourist industry on which so many people in Mexico now depend.

CASE STUDY
ECOTOURISM

In the mountains close to the city of Oaxaca, young Zapotec Indians are creating new employment for themselves. Various projects have been set up in an effort to stop young people from migrating to cities in search of employment. One such project involves students from the small town of Ixtlan. The land has been owned communally by Zapotec Indians for thousands of years.

The young people who live there already know much about the large areas of forest on their traditional lands, and they are now putting that knowledge to great use, learning how to run ecotourism businesses. Several students attending the local university have studied the natural history of their local area and now take ecotourists on weekends away into the forest. The visitors can either mountain bike or hike through the forest to look for rare birds, mammals and insects. One local student has become a specialist on the butterfly species, and he runs tours where he nets butterflies for people to observe.

Ecotourism provides jobs for local people, as well as helping to protect the environment.

GLOSSARY

Aquifer A layer of underground rock that soaks up and stores water.

Biodiversity The variation (diversity) of biological life within an area.

Bolsons River valleys that have no exit to the sea.

Chicle The sticky sap collected from the chicle tree. It is used to make chewing gum.

Conquistador (plural: *conquistadores*) A Spanish word for an adventurer or explorer who sets out to conquer another nation.

Continental plates Large areas of the Earth's crust, floating on top of a layer of molten rock.

Deforestation The clearance of trees, either for timber or for land.

Ecosystem A system that represents the relationships within a community of living things and between this community and their nonliving environment. An ecosystem can be as small as a pond or as large as the Earth.

Ecotourism Tourism that is sensitive to its impact on environments and local populations.

Erosion The removal of soil and rock by natural forces (wind and rain) or people (deforestation).

Fault A line of weakness in the Earth's crust.

Geothermal power Energy derived from the heat contained in rocks deep within the Earth's crust, or from hot springs or volcanoes.

GDP (Gross Domestic Product) The monetary value of goods and services produced by a country in a single year.

GNI (Gross National Income) The monetary value of goods and services produced by a country plus any earnings from overseas in a single year. It used to be called Gross National Product (GNP).

HEP (hydroelectric power) Electricity generated by using the power of water.

Informal economy The part of a nation's economy that is not recorded officially and for which no taxes are paid.

Infrastructure The basic economic foundations of a country such as roads, bridges, communication networks and sewerage systems.

Life expectancy The expected number of years that a person will live.

Malnourished Suffering from lack of food or a poor diet.

Maquiladora A sector of Mexican manufacturing industry that is specifically for the production of foreign brand-named goods for sale abroad.

Megacity A city with a population of more than 10 million.

Mestizo A Spanish word describing people of mixed Indian and European race.

Peninsula A piece of land that is almost entirely surrounded by water.

Plateau (plural: plateaux) A high, flat area of land.

Pre-Hispanic A term describing the time before the arrival of the first Spaniards in 1519.

Rain forest Dense tropical forest with high rainfall.

Services Economic activities that are paid for although nothing is produced, such as tourism and banking.

Smog A combination of the words *smoke* and *fog*, describing a mixture of pollutants in the air.

Temperate climate A climate characterized by mild temperatures.

Tropical climate A climate of constant high temperatures and rainfall, found between the tropics of Cancer and Capricorn.

Urbanization The development and growth of an urban (city) area.

METRIC CONVERSION TABLE

To convert	to	do this
mm (millimeters)	inches	divide by 25.4
cm (centimeters)	inches	divide by 2.54
m (meters)	feet	multiply by 3.281
m (meters)	yards	multiply by 1.094
km (kilometers)	yards	multiply by 1094
km (kilometers)	miles	divide by 1.6093
kilometers per hour	miles per hour	divide by 1.6093
cm^2 (square centimeters)	square inches	divide by 6.452
m^2 (square meters)	square feet	multiply by 10.76
m^2 (square meters)	square yards	multiply by 1.196
km^2 (square kilometers)	square miles	divide by 2.59
km^2 (square kilometers)	acres	multiply by 247.1
hectares	acres	multiply by 2.471
cm^3 (cubic centimeters)	cubic inches	multiply by 16.387
m^3 (cubic meters)	cubic yards	multiply by 1.308
l (liters)	pints	multiply by 2.113
l (liters)	gallons	divide by 3.785
g (grams)	ounces	divide by 28.329
kg (kilograms)	pounds	multiply by 2.205
metric tonnes	short tons	multiply by 1.1023
metric tonnes	long tons	multiply by 0.9842
BTUs (British thermal units)	kWh (kilowatt-hours)	divide by 3,415.3
watts	horsepower	multiply by 0.001341
kWh (kilowatt-hours)	horsepower-hours	multiply by 1.341
MW (megawatts)	horsepower	multiply by 1,341
gigawatts per hour	horsepower per hour	multiply by 1,341,000
°C (degrees Celsius)	°F (degrees Fahrenheit)	multiply by 1.8 then add 32

FURTHER INFORMATION

BOOKS TO READ:

Cory, Steve. *Cities Through Time: Daily Life in Ancient and Modern Mexico City*. Minneapolis: Runestone Press, 1999. Illustrated reference for ages 9 to 12.

Heinrichs, Ann. *A True Book: Mexico*. Danbury, Connecticut: Children's Press, 1997. Illustrated reference for ages 9 to 12.

Ryan, Pam Muñoz. *Esperanza Rising*. New York: Scholastic Press, 2002. A fictional story of thirteen-year-old Esperanza, who must leave her life of privilege in Mexico and immigrate to the United States in the 1930s.

Noble, John, et al. *Mexico*. 8th ed. Footscray, Australia: Lonely Planet Publications Pty. Ltd., 2002. Budget travel guide for travelers of all ages.

Steele, Philip. *The Aztec News*. Cambridge, Massachusetts: Candlewick Press, 2000. Humorous illustrated reference for ages 9 and up.

WEBSITES:

GENERAL INFORMATION:

CIA World Factbook
http://www.cia.gov/cia/publications/factbook/

DEVELOPMENT INFORMATION:

United Nations Development Program (UNDP)
http://www.undp.org/

United Nations Children Fund (UNICEF)
http://www.unicef.org/

WILDLIFE INFORMATION:

World Wildlife Fund — Mexico
http://www.wwf.org.mx/

TOURIST INFORMATION:

Lonely Planet
http://lonelyplanet.com/

USEFUL ADDRESSES:

Mexican Embassy
1911 Pennsylvania Avenue NW
Washington, DC 20006

Mexican Government Tourist Office
2401 W. 6th Street, 5th floor
Los Angeles, CA 90057

Over thousands of years, water rich in minerals has created this spectacular "petrified waterfall" called Hierve El Agua, near Oaxaca City.

Bighorn sheep find sanctuary on the uninhabited islands of the Gulf of California.

The prickly pear cactus is a familiar sight in Mexican deserts. Its fruits are eaten by humans and its stems provide fodder for desert cattle.